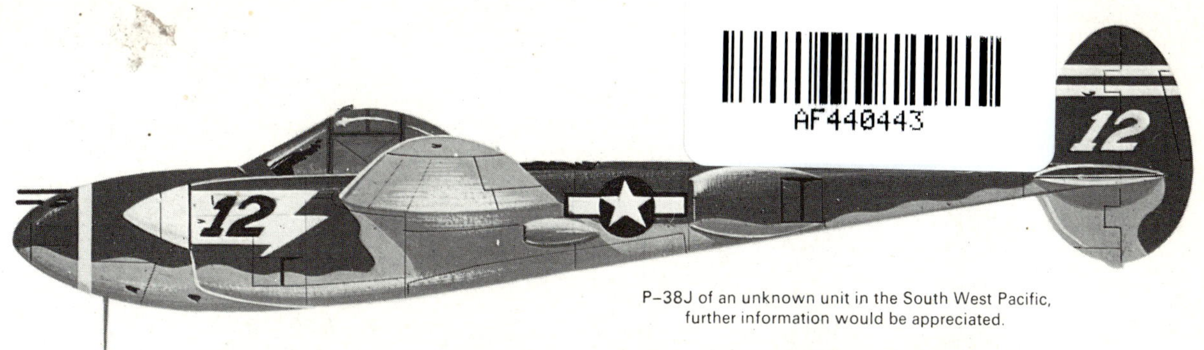

P–38J of an unknown unit in the South West Pacific,
further information would be appreciated.

LOCKHEED P-38 LIGHTNING
IN USAF·FRENCH·ITALIAN·CHINESE NATIONALIST SERVICE

**Illustrated and Compiled by
Richard Ward**

Text by Ernest R. McDowell

ACKNOWLEDGMENTS

Many friends helped with photographs and information to make possible this pictorial survey of the Lightning. My thanks to all who assisted whose names are listed below in alphabetical order. Further information on unidentified units would be appreciated.

G. Apostolo, Peter M. Bowers, Ray E. Bowers, R. Beuschel, G. Cattaneo, J. Cuny, Earl Reinert, E. Munday, J. Sciutti, K. Sumney, E. Vagi, Gibson Vance Jr., United States Air Force, United States Marine Corps, Etablissement Cinematographique des Armees, Imperial War Museum, Italian Air Force.

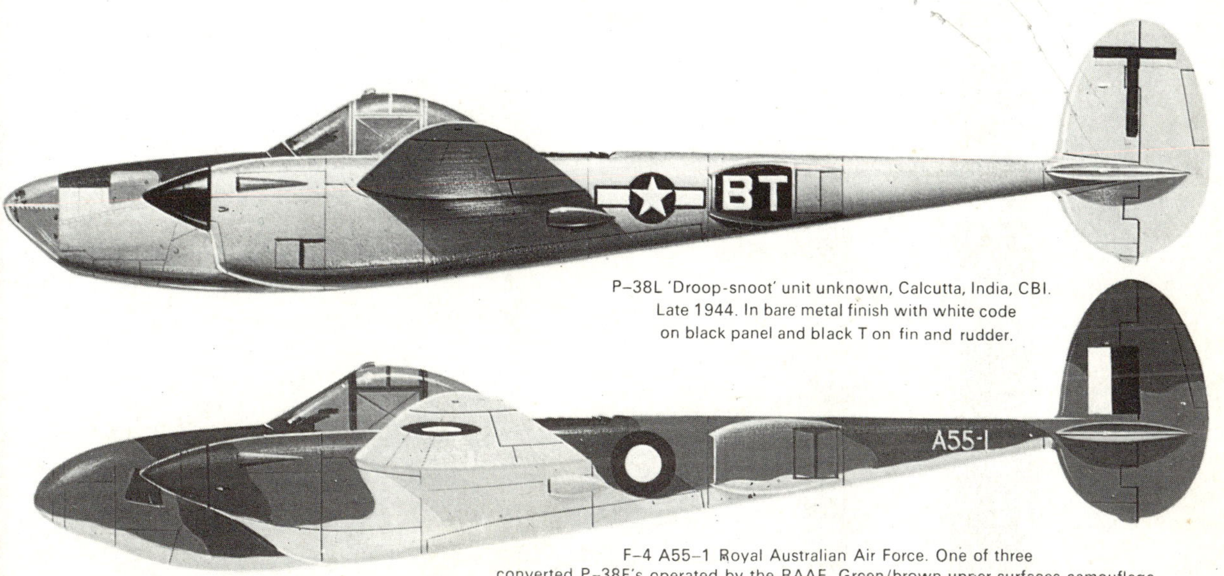

P–38L 'Droop-snoot' unit unknown, Calcutta, India, CBI.
Late 1944. In bare metal finish with white code
on black panel and black T on fin and rudder.

F–4 A55–1 Royal Australian Air Force. One of three
converted P–38E's operated by the RAAF. Green/brown upper surfaces camouflage,
pale blue under surfaces, A55–1 in white, standard white/blue roundels.

PUBLISHED BY
Arco Publishing Company, Inc., 219 Park Avenue South, New York, N.Y. 10003
First Published by Osprey Publications Ltd. and Printed in Great Britain
Library of Congress No. 70-93932 · Library Edition SBN 668-02114-4 · Paperback Edition SBN 668-02113-6

Copyright © Osprey Publications Ltd. 1969

Above: Excellent detail shot of the business end of a Lightning of a training unit of the 3rd Air Force   (USAF)

Below: P-38E (A55-3) EX41-2122, of No. 1 Photo Recon Unit Royal Australian Air Force seen over Northern Australia, 1943. Standard Finish on A/C. Foliage green/earth brown uppers. Sky blue under sides. Serial-white
(R. E. Hourigan via Frank F. Smith)

Like so many Mantis . . . P–38J's of the 55th Fighter Group, 38th Fighter Squadron, 8th Air Force, taking off from Wormingford, Essex, on an escort mission.   (USAF)

LOCKHEED P-38 LIGHTNING

Major Richard Ira Bong, 40 victories, Major Thomas B. McGuire, Jr., 38 victories, Col. Charles H. MacDonald, 27 victories, Gerald Johnson, Tommy Lynch, Robbins, Smith, Dahl, Pierce, DeHaven, the listing of aces who gained all or a part of their victories flying the P-38 could go on and on. Major Bong was the leading American Ace of World War II and all forty of his kills were scored with the P-38.

Despite the impressive totals compiled by the P-38 Aces the aircraft itself saw limited service in that it was used by only 27 groups, contrasted for example by the 58 groups that used the P-47, it did not have the same chance to run up a score. In the ETO the P-51 flew almost twice as many sorties while the P-47 flew almost four times as many sorties as the Lightning in the theater. The P-38 compiled slightly over 2,500 kills in Europe while losing a little over 1,750 aircraft. Its combat mission loss rate of 1.4% per sortie was high for the theater. All told the Lightning groups flew almost 130,000 sorties.

Many of the groups that did fly the P-38 in combat did not fly it for any great length of time before converting to either the Thunderbolt or Mustang. Only 23 groups flew the plane in combat theaters, one of these groups saw no action at all, and a number of the others flew it along with other aircraft at the same time. Most of the P-38 outfits that saw extensive action were in the South Pacific or North Africa.

The end of the war spelt the end of the career of the Lightning. Maintenance costs of a twin-engine fighter are just about double those of a single-engine one. Unlike the Mustang and Thunderbolt the Lightning did not find itself relegated to an Air Guard role. It was instead left to the saws and drop hammers of the scrap dealers. A small number declared as war surplus were picked up by civilian firms to be used in aerial survey, mapping, and photography work. A few others were purchased by racing enthusiasts and entered in the National Air Races in the immediate post war years when they were resumed.

Foreign usage of the P-38 was limited, the Chinese Nationalist Air Force received some Lightnings. The French and Italian Air Forces also were given some P-38s which were used early in the post war years but phased out rather quickly.

The first combat missions and first victory scored by a P-38 were flown from bases in Iceland and the kill was recorded when a Focke-Wulf Kurier was shot down over the Atlantic in August of 1942.

The European Theater of Operations

The Eighth Air Force had a total of seven groups of Lightnings. These were the 1st, 14th, 20th, 55th, 78th, 364th and 479th.

The 1st Fighter Group entered combat with the 8th Air Force on 28 August, 1942. After flying a number of sorties against the low countries and France the 1st was re-assigned to the 12th Air Force and sent to North Africa.

The 14th Group flew anti-submarine and coastal defense patrols on the West Coast of the U.S. operating out of March and Hamilton airfields in California before being sent to England to join the 8th Air Force in October. Serving mainly in the bomber escort role the 14th covered the heavies hitting targets in France but soon joined the 1st Group in North Africa as a part of the 12th Air Force.

The 20th Fighter Group joined the 8th in August of 1943 and went into combat in late December of that year. It kept its P-38s until July of 1944 when it converted to Mustangs.

The 55th Group became a member of the 8th in September of 1943 equipped with the Lightning at the time. First mission was flown on 15 October, 1943, and the Group continued to operate the P-38 until July of 1944.

The 78th Group after training with the P-38 and serving as part of the air defense organization, moved to England and joined the 8th in December of '42 but lost its pilots and aircraft in February of '43 when they were sent to the 12th Air Force. The Group never did fly the P-38 in combat with the 8th as it was replaced with the P-47.

The 364th Group moved from California to England in February of '44 and became operational just 23 days later, on 2 March, 1944. They converted to P-51s in July of '44 after flying their Lightnings in combat less than six months. This Group had a total of 20 aces many of whom scored their first kills with the P-38, one of the leading aces, Lt. Col. Lowell, had at least four kills with the P-38.

The final Lightning group assigned to the 8th was the 479th which joined up in May of 1944 and immediately began flying escort missions which they continued to do until October when they began to convert to P-51s.

Thus while the 8th had seven groups assigned to it, two saw very limited action, the 1st and 14th, and one saw none at all, the 78th. The remaining groups did see quite a bit of combat action and gave a good account of themselves with the Lightning. None of the groups kept the P-38 a full year before converting to other types.

One good use made of the P-38 Groups was assigning them to cover the invasion fleet on D-Day over the Channel as all but the most trigger happy gunners in the convoy could not mistake the Lightnings' silhouette for a German fighter.

The 20th Group won a DUC (Distinguished Unit Citation) for a deep fighter penetration sweep into Germany to shoot up airfields and other targets of opportunity. This was flown on 8 April, 1944. They shot up a number of 'dromes, beat off an attack by defending fighters and proceeded to shoot up oil supplies, rolling stock and locomotives and anything else that found itself in their path on the way back. The Group won the nickname of " Loco Group " for its successes in working over the railroads of Europe and shooting up locomotives and rolling stock.

The other group to win a DUC was the 479th which was awarded their citation for a series of missions flown during the period of 18 August through 5 September, 1944. They destroyed a large number of enemy aircraft on the ground on aerodromes in France during the period and, in a large aerial duel over the Munster area, shot down many more.

The 55th and 364th failed to win any citations while flying the P-38.

The 9th Air Force had only three Lightning Groups assigned to it, these were the 367th, 370th and 474th.

The 367th Group became a part of the 9th in April of 1944 and flew the Lightning until February of '45 when it converted to the Thunderbolt. Taking up duties similar to those already described for the 8th Air Force Groups, the 367th flew Channel cover on D-Day and then continued to support the invasion forces during the entire month of June. In July the Group moved to the European mainland and assumed a purely tactical role. They won a DUC for a double mission flown on 25 August when they shot up air strips at Rosieries, Clastres and Peronne, destroying a number of aircraft both on the ground and in the air. Taking off again the same day they flew a fighter sweep of over 800 miles to hit more aerodromes at Bourges, Dijon and Cognac.

The 370th joined the 9th in February of '44 but did not go on combat operations until May 1st. After the usual breaking in period of sorties they were a part of the D-Day fighter cover over the Channel and then flew armed recon missions over the Cotentin Peninsula the rest of June in support of the invasion forces. They also supplied cover for the airborne assault on Holland in September. Their DUC was earned for carrying out a close support mission in the Hurtgen Forest area on 2nd December pressing home a napalm bomb attack in the face of heavy anti-aircraft and small arms fire on the village of Bergstein. The attack was mounted under the worst possible set of weather conditions but it did not deter the group one bit. After taking part in the Battle of the Bulge they converted to the Mustang.

The 474th Group arrived in England in March of 1944 and was assigned to the 9th Air Force. They began combat operations on 25 April, 1944, with the usual patrol of the French coast. This group was selected to provide night cover over the Channel for the D-Day Invasion Forces and flew dive-bombing missions in support of the landing the next day and in all probability saw more real action than most groups in that respect. The group moved to the European continent in August and assumed an almost exclusive ground close support role. Their DUC was won on 23 August, 1944, when they came across a large number of German Panzer units massed along the Seine River in the Falaise-Argentan area attempting to cross the river in an orderly withdrawal. Going on to the attack at once they repeatedly dive-bombed and strafed the German forces disrupting their retreat and throwing it into mass confusion. This action enabled the pursuing Allied forces to further decimate or capture a large number of Germans with their vital equipment. This Group was the only one to retain its P-38s until VE-Day. They participated in the airborne attack on Holland, the Battle of the Bulge, the crossing of the Rhine, and they remained in action until the war ended. The Group was also cited by the Belgian Government and awarded the Belgian Fourragere.

The Mediterranean Theater of Operations

The 12th Air Force initially had four P-38 Groups but lost three of them to the 15th Air Force at a later date. For the purpose of this text all will be dealt with at this

Line-up of natural metal P–38's, note cover plate on turbo-supercharger.   (USAF)

Above: YP–38 in flight.

Above: P–38 showing modification to radiator intake, 1941.

Above: P–38 coming in to land, note US Army under wings.

Below: P–38 during 1941 War Games.

Below: P–38D, November 1941.

Above: P–38D, November 1941.

Above: P–322 with RAF serial AE992.

Above: P–38E, 1943

Above: P–38F, 1944.   Below: RP–38, April 1943.

Below: P–38L, 1945.   (Photos Peter M. Bowers)

Above: F-4, North Africa 1943.

Above: F-4A, India 1943.

Above: F-5E, converted P-38J.

Above & below: P-38L with F-5 nose designation on fuselage.

Below: F-5G, Shanghai 1945.   (Photos Peter M. Bowers)

point rather than trying to break them down into two separate groups covering activities in each air force. The 12th started with the 1st, 14th, 82nd and 350th Groups, the 350th remained with the 12th until the end of the war.

The 1st Group came to the 12th, as previously mentioned, from England, equipped with the P-38 which they flew until the end of the war. They won three DUCs. The first for a successful strafing attack on massed enemy aircraft that had been brought up to oppose the anticipated landings at Salerno. The action took place on 25 August, 1943. Less than a week later, on 30 August to be exact, they picked up a second DUC for fighting off a massed attack by enemy fighters on the heavy bombers they were escorting thus enabling the bombers to inflict heavy damage on the marshalling yards at Aversa. They supported the actual Salerno invasion in September and were re-assigned to the 15th Air Force in November. Their third DUC came on 18 May, 1944, when they provided withdrawal support for the bombers returning from a raid on the Ploesti oil fields. They finished out the war by providing air cover for the Anzio beach landings, the Invasion of Southern France, and continued to escort the heavy bombers into Germany.

The 14th Group's record is almost a duplicate of the record of the 1st Group in that they went to England as a part of the 8th, were re-assigned to the 12th and arrived in North Africa on 11 November, 1942, and were finally sent to the 15th in November of 1943. They also flew the P-38 for the entire war. Missions were very similar to the 1st Group's. They won their DUC on 2 April, 1944, for keeping a large force of enemy fighters at bay while the bombers they were protecting hit ball-bearing works in Austria.

The 82nd Group was sent to Northern Ireland in October of 1942 for additional training on the P-38 but were not assigned to any air force in particular until being ordered to join the 12th in North Africa in December of 1942 to reinforce the fighter groups being hard pressed at the time. They won a pair of DUCs before being re-assigned to the 15th in November of '43. The first DUC was awarded for a low level strafing mission on 25 August, 1943. Their target was a large concentration of enemy aircraft on the various airfields in the Foggia complex. The second DUC came a week later when they saved a large bomber formation from annihilation on 2 September, 1943. They spotted the heavy bombers under a viscious attack by a large number of Nazi fighters and bored in at once to drive them off. The bombers had failed to make contact with their withdrawal escort after a raid on the marshalling yards at Naples and were without protection. They earned their third DUC as a part of the 15th Air Force on 10 June, 1944, for a dive-bombing attack on the Ploesti oil complex. The 82nd continued flying P-38s until the war's end.

The 350th Group followed the others from England to the 12th in North Africa, however, this group was never entirely equipped with the Lightning, they also flew P-39s and P-40s but they spent the rest of the war with the 12th. Whether they rightfully can be counted as a P-38 group is naturally debatable. Since so far as can be determined, the Bell aircraft always outnumbered the P-38, this group will be passed over with just this mention.

A wing mission laid on the 2nd of April, 1944, will best serve to illustrate the type of action the P-38s in the Mediterranean found themselves engaged in. The 82nd Group was flying cover to a formation of heavy bombers. The time was approximately 10.15 hours. Suddenly a group estimated at about 50 Me-109s, FW-190s and MC-202s made a head on pass at the 82nd and unlike most being encountered at the time these appeared ready to mix it with the P-38s. Their eagerness was brought on by the fact that another large formation was stalking the bombers from a position high above and it was their job to draw off the 82nd and thus expose the bombers to attack by their top group. The 82nd held their station but did manage to pick off three of the attacking force with quick snap shots. The top group did not attack.

The 325th Group flying P-47s took over from the 82nd at 10.45 hours and they too were subjected to the same

P–38H being refuelled at Wormingford, see colour illustration A1. 20th Fighter Group, 55th Fighter Squadron, 8th AF.   (Ray E. Bowers)

sort of tactics by 21 Me-109s and again three of the 109s were shot down and the bombers protected.

The 1st Group's Lightnings showed up to relieve the 325th promptly at 11.30 hours and were set upon shortly thereafter by 16 more Nazi fighters, but these lacking a top group, attempted to by-pass them and get at the bombers. A thirty minute dog-fight ensued and more Germans showed up and joined in the battle, hitting both the bombers and their escorting P-38s. The 1st Group shot down eight Germans before the 14th Group's Lightnings arrived at high noon, again right on schedule, to find their comrades engaging from 70—75 enemy fighters. They immediately joined the action with a will and shot down 18 of the enemy planes. The totals for this mission were 32 enemy fighters shot down, six listed as probables and eight more as damaged. The USAAF lost a lone P-38 which had to make a belly landing near its base on the return flight. The bombers got through to the target, the ball-bearing works at Steyr, Austria, and made a successful bombing attack on it.

The Lightnings were often pressed into service as bombers when the occasion demanded it. Such an occasion arose on 10 June, 1944, and involved P-38s of the 82nd Group. They took off at dawn, led by Lt. Col. William P. Litton, and headed their bomb laden craft at tree top level towards Yugoslavia. Flying along the Danube until they reached a pre-determined point near Budapest they pivoted on it and headed directly for Ploesti. The 1st Fighter Group was flying top cover throughout the mission.

Reaching the target area they zoomed up in a fast climb to gain altitude for a diving attack on the Romano American Oil Refineries which had managed to escape any serious damage in other raids by the heavy bombers. Boring down through smoke screens, intense flak, and enemy fighters they ignored each in turn until after releasing their bomb loads. Hits were scored on the all-important cracking plant and in the area of the distillation unit and boiler houses. Someone hit a large storage tank which exploded and sent flaming fuel over the area.

Lt. Col. Ben A. Mason, Jr., had been forced to ignore a Me-110 that had attempted to intercept him on the way in but on the way out he encountered a 110 and shot him down, whether this was the same one is not known. He added two locomotives and several other vehicles and kept shooting up targets on the way back until his ammo was exhausted. Other pilots added eight more locomotives, and vehicles that were in the path of their return route. The 1st Fighter Group which had been acting as top cover now got its chance and destroyed 24 enemy aircraft that had responded to the call for air cover from those on the ground.

Possibly the worst day of the war from a loss standpoint came on D-Day during the invasion of Southern France. The 1st and 14th lost a combined total of 23 P-38s and almost the same number of pilots along with other casualties as a result of the operation. The 14th flew a total of 18 missions during the day but this was topped by the 21 flown by the 1st Group. The Groups flew a total of 1,033 sorties during the landings and destroyed 224 pieces of enemy equipment.

The 82nd Group now equipped with the droop snoot P-38 complete with a bombardier now began to fly high altitude missions in place of bombers. The 15th Air Force press release announcing this new type of mission was as follows:

" 15th Air Force in Italy — For the first time in history of the MTO, high altitude bombing by P-38 Lightning type airplanes was undertaken on August 29th, when a 15th Air Force Group led by Col. C. T. Edwinson, dropped a 15-ton bomb load on a railroad bridge in Northern Italy near Latisana.

" After dropping their bombs the P-38s conducted a sweep in which they destroyed six locomotives, damaged three others, and strafed a number of tank cars and rolling stock. No flak or enemy fighters were encountered.

" The bombs were well concentrated in the target area as recon planes were in the area during the bombing and filmed the attacks by the P-38s. Bombs were dropped from an altitude of 15,000 feet."

Left: P–38H, 20th FG, 55th FS, aircraft letter Z, serial 267052.   (via E. Munday)

Below: P–38J of the 55th FS, belly landed at Kingscliffe, Northants.   (Ray E. Bowers)

Jeanne' complete with 'sharkmouth' and white wing tips somewhat embarrassed, see colour illustration A3.   (Ray E. Bowers)

Some missions of this type produced excellent results, others resulted in practically dry runs and the raids were finally discontinued in favor of the conventional types.

The experiences of a pair of Lightning pilots on a low level strafing mission is a testimonial to the ruggedness of the P-38. Lt. John M. Hurley lost about four feet of his right wing tip when a 40 mm shell hit it and the wing tank was riddled by 20 mm shells. He looked to his flight leader for possible assistance. The leader, Lt. James A. Eddins, was in even worse shape. His P-38 had taken a direct hit on the nose, knocking out all guns and exploding the ammo. Bits of metal blown off had hit the tips of the left prop, damaging it and making the engine run rough. Other pieces had damaged the stabilizer. A direct hit had knocked out the right engine. The two damaged planes turned for home with a third acting as escort. Eddins had a fight on his hands. His plane had a tendency to shake, stall, and try to roll over and spin. The best speed he could manage was about 120 mph. To make it worse he was down on the deck. Mountains between him and his base made it imperative that he get up to at least 13,000 feet. The process took almost an hour and he only got up to 11,000, gaining altitude a little at a time he would climb, level off, nose down a bit to avoid a spin, then repeat the process over again. Finally he made it through a pass, nosed down slightly and built his speed up to 155 mph and limped into base.

Lt. Hurley with the missing wing tip and no fuel in the right wing tank made it back with only a slightly less amount of difficulty. Both pilots were very thankful for the strong airplane that Lockheed had produced.

The 14th Group possessed in Lt. Col. Charles D. Chitty, Groups Ops Officer, and Lt. Col. Hugh A. Griffith, a squadron CO, the top locomotive busters in the theater. Their totals of over 30 each made them top " Loco-Busters " in the area.

The Pacific Theater of Operations

The 5th Air Force possessed four P-38 groups, the 8th, 35th, 475th and the 49th, the top P-38 group of the war. The 8th Group initially flew P-39s and P-40s adding P-38s by May of '44 and finished out the war with them. They soon phased out the other aircraft so that by the time they received a DUC on 26 December, 1944, they were flying only the P-38. This award came for the part they played in routing a strong Japanese naval force off Mindoro. They repeatedly attacked the ships and their strafing attacks were pressed home so fiercely that the ships were forced to scatter and eventually turn back.

The 35th went onto operations with a mixture of P-38s and P-39s which they flew until switched over to P-47s late in '43. Although not involved in any outstanding mission, they flew protective patrols, escorted bombers, and handled close support duties well during the period.

The 49th Group went into combat equipped with P-40s and began their conversion to the P-38 with the 9th Squadron. In September of 1944 the entire group had Lightnings and kept them until VJ-Day. The group earned a DUC with its P-38s on the strength of an intensive campaign in the Philippines, in the Leyte area, during which they destroyed a large number of Japanese aircraft. The 49th had over 40 Aces on its roster. Major Bong gained 23 of his 40 kills flying with the group and won the Congressional Medal of Honor while flying with them. At one time or another just about every high scoring Ace in the area flew with the 49th.

The 475th was the only P-38 group in the 5th Air Force to be activated in the theater. It thus was the only group to begin and end its career flying Lightnings and was mostly composed of veterans from the other groups. Like the 49th, the 475th possessed a Medal of Honor

'Mama's Boy' a P–38J of the 20th FG, 55th FS, in full D-Day markings, see colour illustration A4.   (USAF)

P-38J, K of the 55th FS.   (via E. Munday)

P-38J, 77th FS, note white wing tips, code LC-T.   (Ray E. Bowers)

winner in Major Thomas B. McGuire, Jr. The 475th received three DUCs, the first for an escort mission to Wewak in August '43 when they not only protected the bombers in their care but also shot down most of the Japanese fighters that attempted to break up the raid. DUC number two came for their role in beating off a large Japanese fighter force that was attacking shipping in Oro Bay in October of '43. The third DUC was won for extended operations during the initial stages of the Philippines Campaign during October-December 1944.

The 7th Air Force had a lone Lightning Group, the 21st, in its command. This group started with P-39s and switched to the P-38 while serving as a part of the Hawaiian Islands Defense in 1944, They saw no combat, other than routine patrols, as a group. The 531st Squadron, however, was detached and sent to join the 318th Group to serve as long range escorts for the B-24s and B-29s now hitting Truk and Iwo Jima. The 36 Lightnings flew to their new base with the pilots thinking that they would be a fourth squadron in the group. Instead they were split up and 12 P-38s were attached to each of the three squadrons.

The 13th Air Force had two Lockheed Groups, the 18th and 347th. The 18th had been all but wiped out at Pearl Harbor and was re-equipped with P-38s and assigned to the 13th. Here again they did not have enough to completely outfit the group so it also flew P-39s, P-61s and P-70s. A move to New Guinea in August of '44 resulted in the entire group getting Lightnings which they retained until the war's end. They won a DUC for shooting up a Jap convoy attempting to reinforce their troops at Leyte. The date was 10 November, 1944.

Like the 18th, the 347th began to operate some P-38s from Guadalcanal in February of '43. They escorted bombers hitting targets on various islands within their range. Their move to New Guinea also resulted in a complete change-over to P-38s. The group now began escorting bombers to the Celebes, Borneo, Ceram and Halmahera. Their DUC came for a series of raids carried out at long range over water to Makassar in the Celebes in November of '44.

The China-Burma-India Theater of Operations

The CBI was similar in some respects to the MTO in that the Lightnings of the 10th Air Force were transferred to the 14th Air Force and both will be covered here as a single unit. The 10th started with three P-38 groups, the 33rd, 51st and 80th.

The 33rd was a seasoned group that had seen action in the Western Desert flying P-40s. The 33rd moved to India in February of '44 and joined the 10th Air Force. They were equipped with P-38s. Missions were flown in Burma and it was then re-assigned to the 14th but continued to operate in the same area until the war ended.

The 51st arrived in India in March of '42 equipped with P-40s. It moved to China in October of '43 and was then re-assigned to the 14th and received some P-38s, using a mixture of Lightnings and Warhawks until re-equipped with Mustangs in 1945. The assigned role of tactical missions prevented it from rolling up a score of kills.

The 80th Group became operational in September 1943 flying a mixture of P-38s and P-40s and was the only one of the three to remain with the 10th the entire war. A DUC was awarded for their role in preventing a large Japanese bomber force from raiding the vital oil refinery in Assam, India, on 27 March, 1944, when they broke up the formations and shot down most of the bombers.

Other areas in which the P-38 operated

The 11th Air Force in the Aleutians included one P-38 group, the 343rd but like so many others it also included a number of P-40s in the earlier days. The group was under the command of Lt. Col. John S. Chenault, the son of the famed AVG Flying Tiger Commander. Stationed at Elmendorf Field they flew patrols, dive-bombed and strafed Jap camps on Kiska and although their last combat mission was flown in October of '43 they remained in Alaska until the war ended.

An oddity was the 32nd Group which operated some P-38s in the Panama Canal Zone along with various other types from May of '42 until November of '43. Though this group should have been a part of the 6th Air Force it is not listed as such in the records.

The four other P-38 groups in existence were all assigned to the 4th Air Force in the Western half of the U.S. as training groups. These included the 360th, 473rd and 329th. Their duty was to train pilots for combat units.

To sum up the Lightning, it enjoyed a highly successful career as a fighter, saw service as the F4 and F5 in the photo recon version, was modified to carry a bombardier in the so called droop snoot version or a radar operator as a night fighter. They hung bombs on it to make it a dive-bomber and level-bomber and even hung a couple of torpedoes on one as an experiment.

It seems that the name the German ground pounders hung on the old bird fit her best. "Der Gabelschwanz Teufel," "The Fork Tailed Devil." As one ex-Lightning Ace put it, it was one "Helluva good ship to fly and it did a Helluva good job."

Nose detail of 'Gentle Annie', see colour illustration B2. (Ray E. Bowers)

Above: 'Murph III' of the 20th FG, 55th FS, code KI–V.　(USAF)

Above: 'Jeanne' of the 20th FG, 55th FS, score markings white on black panel, see colour illustration A5.　(USAF)
Below: 'Dossie' of an unknown 8th AF unit.　(USAF)

Below: P–38J of an unknown 8th AF unit, note coloured rudder.　(USAF)

Nice shot of a P–38J with everything down coming into land. Unit unknown. (USAF)

P–38L 'Droop-snoot' of the 20th Fighter Group, 77th Fighter Squadron, 8th AF. Note white wing fillet, see colour illustration A6.   (USAF)

Left: P–38J, 20th Fighter Group, 77th Fighter Squadron, 8th AF. Serial 268171.
(Ray E. Bowers)

Right: Flak damaged P–38J of an unknown unit after forced-landing at Manston. Note oil saturated cowl and undercart.
(Ray E. Bowers)

Perched high on the edge of the 'White Cliffs of Dover' with the drink beneath the tail booms, this sort of thing made rhubarb and prunes quite unnecessary to keep things moving.   (Ray E. Bowers)

Above: P-38J, 364th Fighter Group, 383rd Fighter Squadron, 8th Air Force, after forced-landing at Manston. (Ray E. Bowers)

Left: Second W of the 384th Fighter Squadron, 364th Fighter Group, also forced-landed at Manston. (Ray E. Bowers)

Right: P-38J, 364th Fighter Group, 385th Fighter Squadron, note flak damaged port spinner. Code 5E-H, serial painted out, white triangle on fin and rudder. (Ray E. Bowers)

Above & below: P-38J, 364th FG, 385th FS, 8th AF. See front cover illustration. (Ray E. Bowers)

Left: P–38J with flak damaged flap at Manston, unit unknown, note coloured rudder. (Ray E. Bowers)

Right: P–38J probably of the 364th FG, 385th FS, 8th AF. (Ray E. Bowers)

Left: P–38J of the 479th Fighter Group, 436th Fighter Squadron, 8th Air Force, the correct code for this squadron is 9B during the time of the P–51, reason for the reversed code is not known. (Ray E. Bowers)

Below: Good nose detail shot of a P–38J, unit unknown. (Ray E. Bowers)

Above: P–38H, 55th Fighter Group, 343rd Fighter Squadron, 8th AF, coming in to land at Wormingford, Essex, note blue/white wheel disc.   (USAF)

Above: P–38H, 55th Fighter Group, 338th Fighter Squadron, warming up at Bassingbourne, base of the 91st Bomb Group for a fighter escort mission.   (USAF)

Left: P–38H of the 55th Fighter Group, 38th Fighter Squadron, forced-landed at Manston.   (Ray E. Bowers)

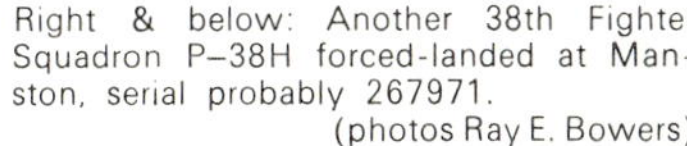

Right & below: Another 38th Fighter Squadron P–38H forced-landed at Manston, serial probably 267971.
(photos Ray E. Bowers)

Above: Red-nosed P–38J, 55th FG, 338th FS, see colour illustration B6. T on the inside of fin and rudder.   (Ray E. Bowers)

Above: 'Janet' a P–38J of the 338th FS, see colour illustration C1. V on inside of fin and rudder.   (Ray E. Bowers)

Above: P–38J, 55th Fighter Group, 343rd Fighter Squadron, not quite making it back to Manston after being hit in the starboard engine over Europe. (Ray E. Bowers)

Left: P–38J nose detail and nose-art, unit unknown. (Ray E. Bowers)

Above: Nice flying shot of P-38J's of the 364th Fighter Group, 383rd Fighter Squadron, 8th Air Force.   (IWM)
Below: Three P-38J's of the 55th Fighter Group, 38th Fighter Squadron, 8th Air Force.   (USAF)

Nice plan view shot of a F–5E probably of the 10th Photo Recon Group, 9th Air Force, flying over the coastline near Ostend, Belgium. May 1945. (USAF)

Above: P–38J, 370th Fighter Group, 401st Fighter Squadron, 9th Air Force, on the former Luftwaffe night-fighter base at Florennes, Belgium (USAF)

Below: P–38J's of the 370th Fighter Group taxying out for take-off on a ground attack mission against German targets, Florennes, Belgium. (USAF)

Above: Very colourful P–38J of the 370th Fighter Group, 485th Fighter Squadron, coming in to land with a dead engine after being damaged during a ground attack mission, Florennes, Belgium. See colour illustration C4. (USAF)

Right: P–38L 'Pathfinder' with BTO (bomb-through-overcast) radar in bulbous nose. Probably of the 67th Tac Recon Group, 9th Air Force, ETO.

Below: 9th Air Force P–38L 'Pathfinder' coming in to land on a B–24 field in England, unit unknown. (USAF)

Fine flying shot of a P–38J of the 1st Fighter Group, 27th Fighter Squadron, 15th Air Force, Italy, MTO.   (USAF)

...nificient close-up of the P-38J shown on the facing page. 1st Fighter Group, 27th Fighter Squadron, 15th Air ..., Italy, MTO. (USAF)

Above: P–38F of the 1st Fighter Group, 94th Fighter Squadron, 12th Air Force, Algeria/Tunisia, MTO.   (Ken Sumney via J. Sciutti)
Below: Neat formation by the 1st Fighter Group, 27th Fighter Squadron, 15th Air Force, Italy, MTO. Serial of 12 424217.   (USAF)

Above: Very interesting nose markings on a 1st FG, 27th FS, P—38F in Italy. Note the 'Diving Eagle' of the 27th FS, 3 Swastikas, 89 escort missions and 45 bombing missions, further information on this aircraft would be appreciated. (USAF)

Below: Cockpit and gunsight detail of a P—38J of the 1st Fighter Group.   (USAF)

Above & below: F–4C's of the 90th Photographic Reconnaissance Wing, 12/15th Air Forces, Italy. MTO. See colour illustration D6. (USAF)

Above three pictures: F–5E's of an unidentified unit in Italy, further information would be appreciated.
(Peter M. Bowers)

Akeno Training School
1938–1942

Akeno Training School
1942–1943

Akeno Training School
1943–1944

Akeno Air Training Division
Instructor Squad
1944–1945

Shimoshizu Flying School
1941–1944

Kumagaya Flying School
1938–1945

Hamamatsu Flying School
1941–1944

Hokota Flying School
1940–1944

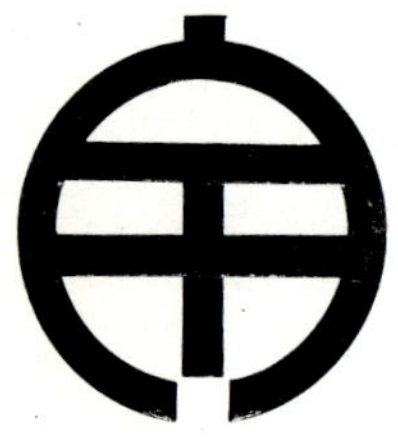

Utsonomia Flying School
1940–1944

Tachiarai Flying School
1940–1945

Army Air Communication School
1940–1945

Army Air Academy
1940–1945

Tokorosawa Air Maintenance School
1943–1944

Hitachi Air Training Division
Instructor Squad
1944–1945

Mito Flying School
1940–1943

107th Pre-Combat Training Company
1943

39th Flight Training Company
Yokoshiba Airfield
1945

Unidentified Flight Training Company
Kallang Airfield, Singapore

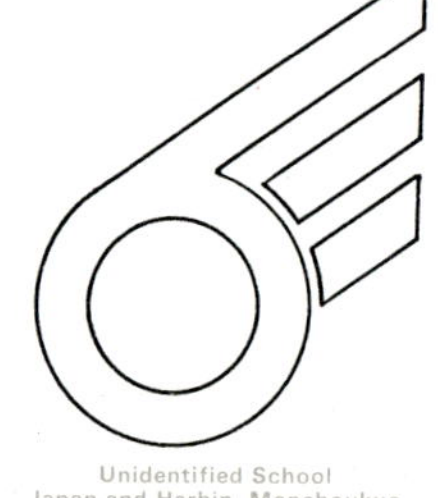

Unidentified School
Japan and Harbin, Manchoukuo
Late 1944–early 1945

12th Combat Training Company
1943

Published by ARCO PUBLISHING COMPANY, INC., 219 Park Avenue South, N.Y., N.Y. 10003. Printed in Great Britain.

© WARD

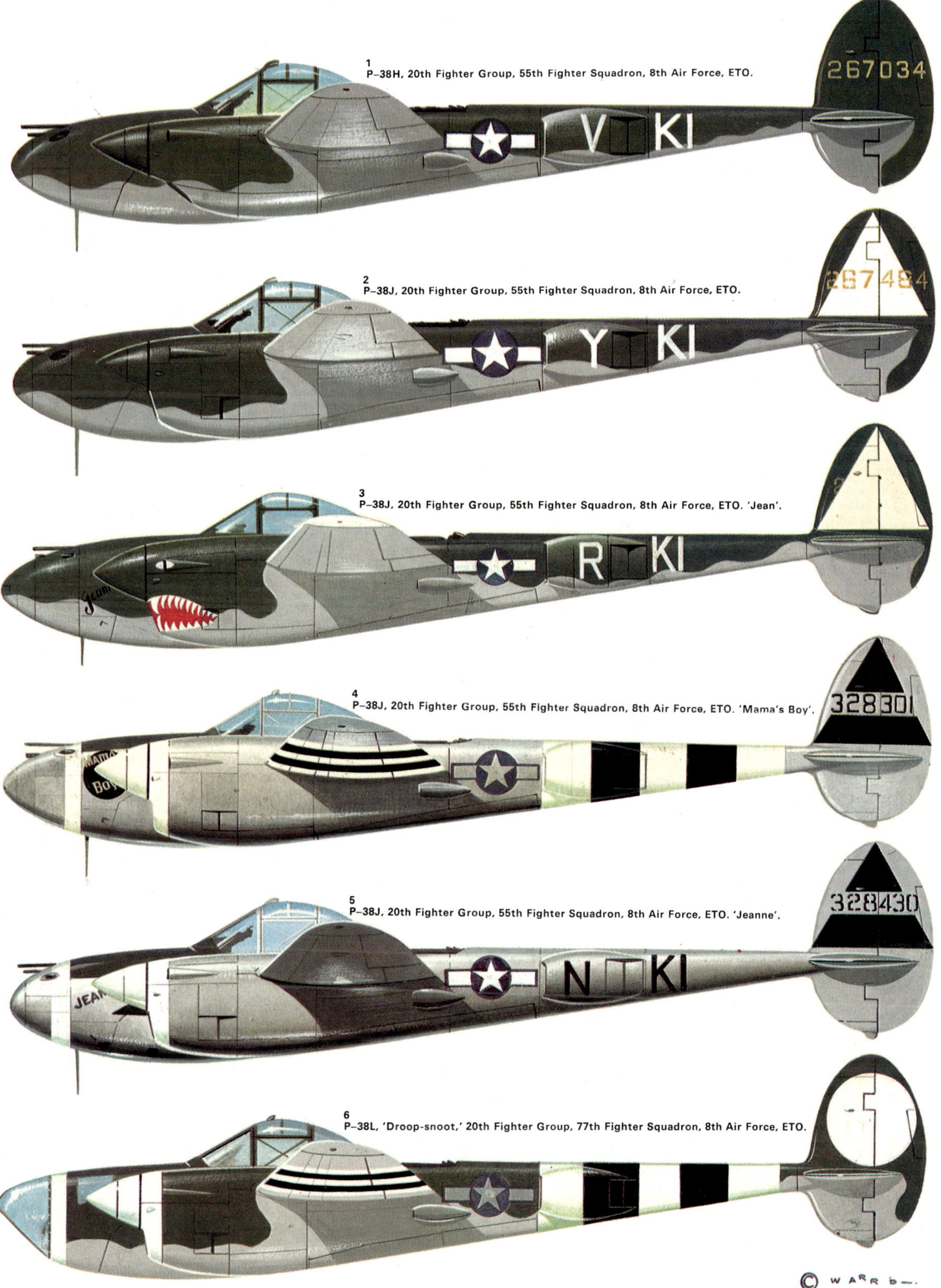

1 P-38H, 20th Fighter Group, 55th Fighter Squadron, 8th Air Force, ETO.

2 P-38J, 20th Fighter Group, 55th Fighter Squadron, 8th Air Force, ETO.

3 P-38J, 20th Fighter Group, 55th Fighter Squadron, 8th Air Force, ETO. 'Jean'.

4 P-38J, 20th Fighter Group, 55th Fighter Squadron, 8th Air Force, ETO. 'Mama's Boy'.

5 P-38J, 20th Fighter Group, 55th Fighter Squadron, 8th Air Force, ETO. 'Jeanne'.

6 P-38L, 'Droop-snoot,' 20th Fighter Group, 77th Fighter Squadron, 8th Air Force, ETO.

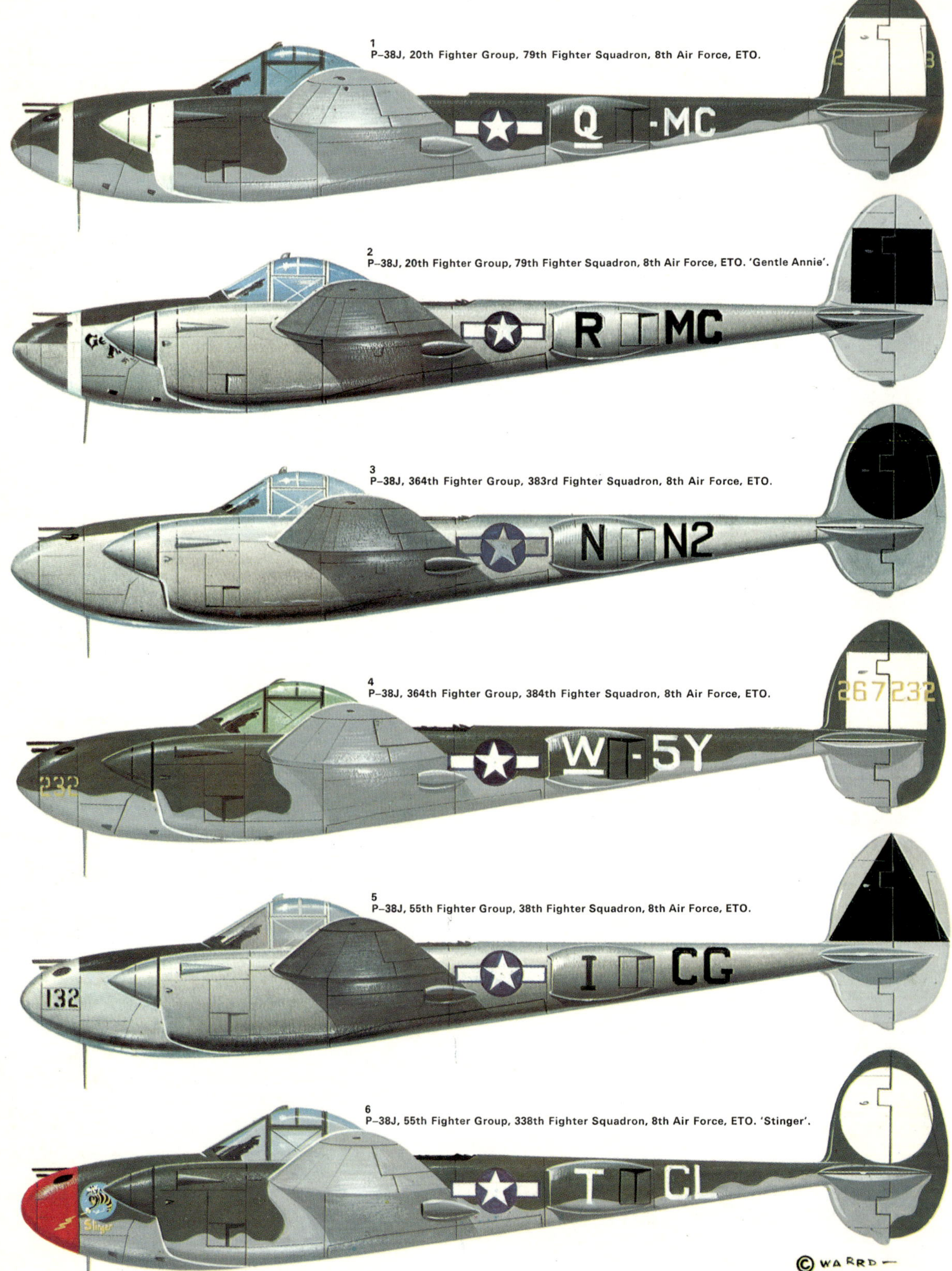

B
1
P-38J, 20th Fighter Group, 79th Fighter Squadron, 8th Air Force, ETO.
Q-MC
2
P-38J, 20th Fighter Group, 79th Fighter Squadron, 8th Air Force, ETO. 'Gentle Annie'.
R-MC
3
P-38J, 364th Fighter Group, 383rd Fighter Squadron, 8th Air Force, ETO.
N-N2
4
P-38J, 364th Fighter Group, 384th Fighter Squadron, 8th Air Force, ETO.
W-5Y
267232
5
P-38J, 55th Fighter Group, 38th Fighter Squadron, 8th Air Force, ETO.
I-CG
6
P-38J, 55th Fighter Group, 338th Fighter Squadron, 8th Air Force, ETO. 'Stinger'.
T-CL
Stinger
© WARRD

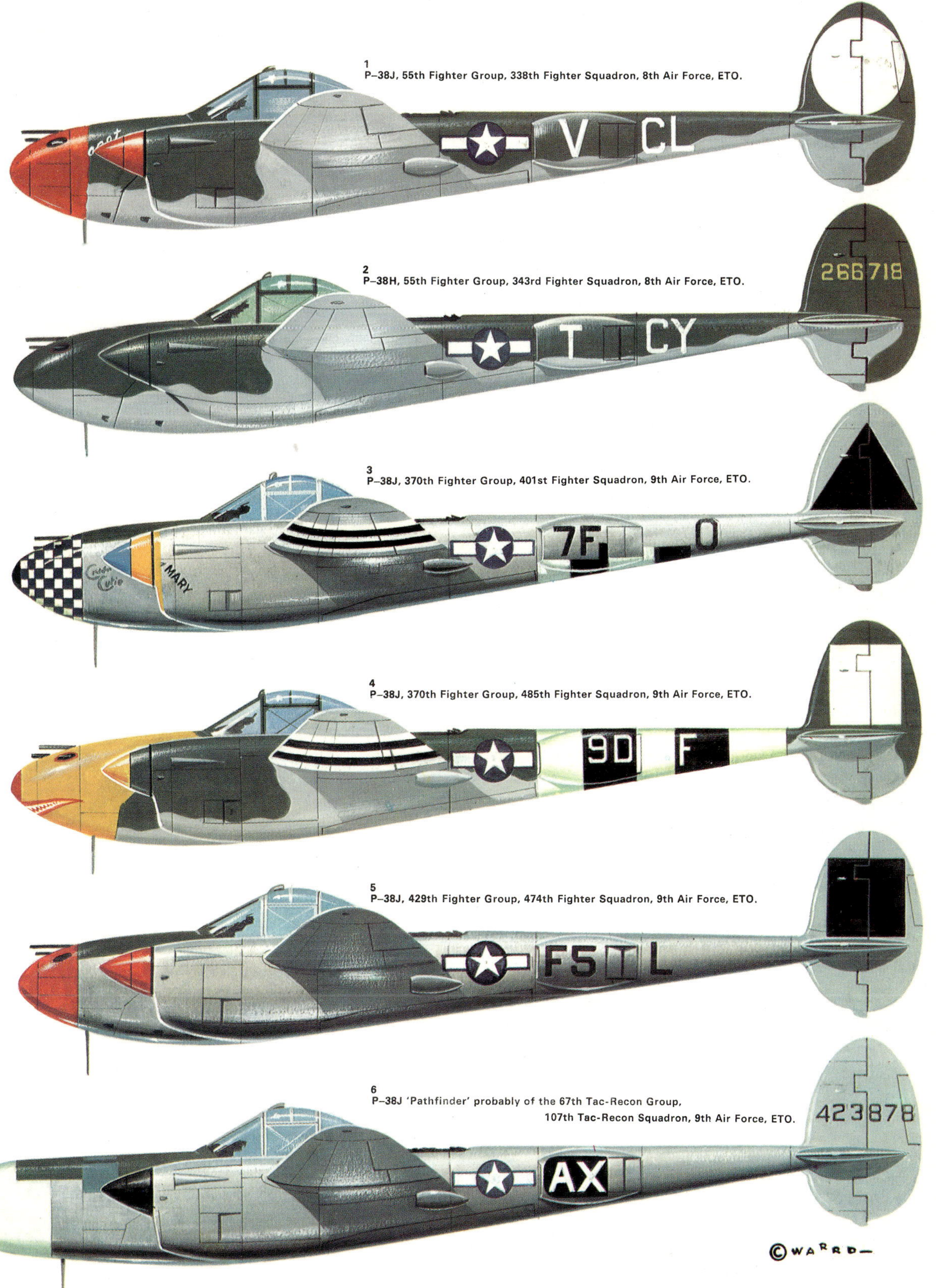

1 P–38J, 55th Fighter Group, 338th Fighter Squadron, 8th Air Force, ETO.

2 P–38H, 55th Fighter Group, 343rd Fighter Squadron, 8th Air Force, ETO.

3 P–38J, 370th Fighter Group, 401st Fighter Squadron, 9th Air Force, ETO.

4 P–38J, 370th Fighter Group, 485th Fighter Squadron, 9th Air Force, ETO.

5 P–38J, 429th Fighter Group, 474th Fighter Squadron, 9th Air Force, ETO.

6 P–38J 'Pathfinder' probably of the 67th Tac-Recon Group,
107th Tac-Recon Squadron, 9th Air Force, ETO.

D

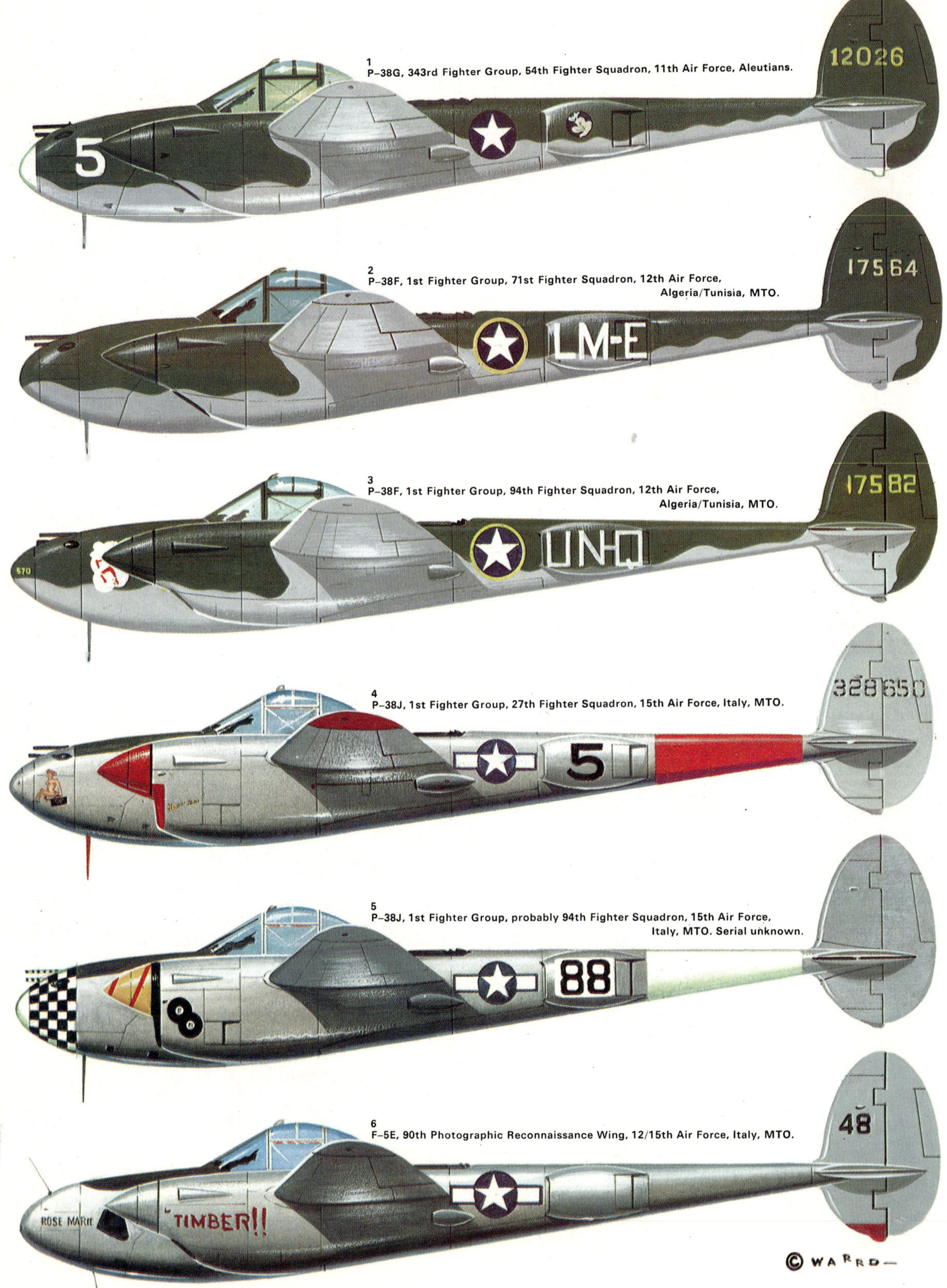

1 P-38G, 343rd Fighter Group, 54th Fighter Squadron, 11th Air Force, Aleutians.

2 P-38F, 1st Fighter Group, 71st Fighter Squadron, 12th Air Force, Algeria/Tunisia, MTO.

3 P-38F, 1st Fighter Group, 94th Fighter Squadron, 12th Air Force, Algeria/Tunisia, MTO.

4 P-38J, 1st Fighter Group, 27th Fighter Squadron, 15th Air Force, Italy, MTO.

5 P-38J, 1st Fighter Group, probably 94th Fighter Squadron, 15th Air Force, Italy, MTO. Serial unknown.

6 F-5E, 90th Photographic Reconnaissance Wing, 12/15th Air Force, Italy, MTO.

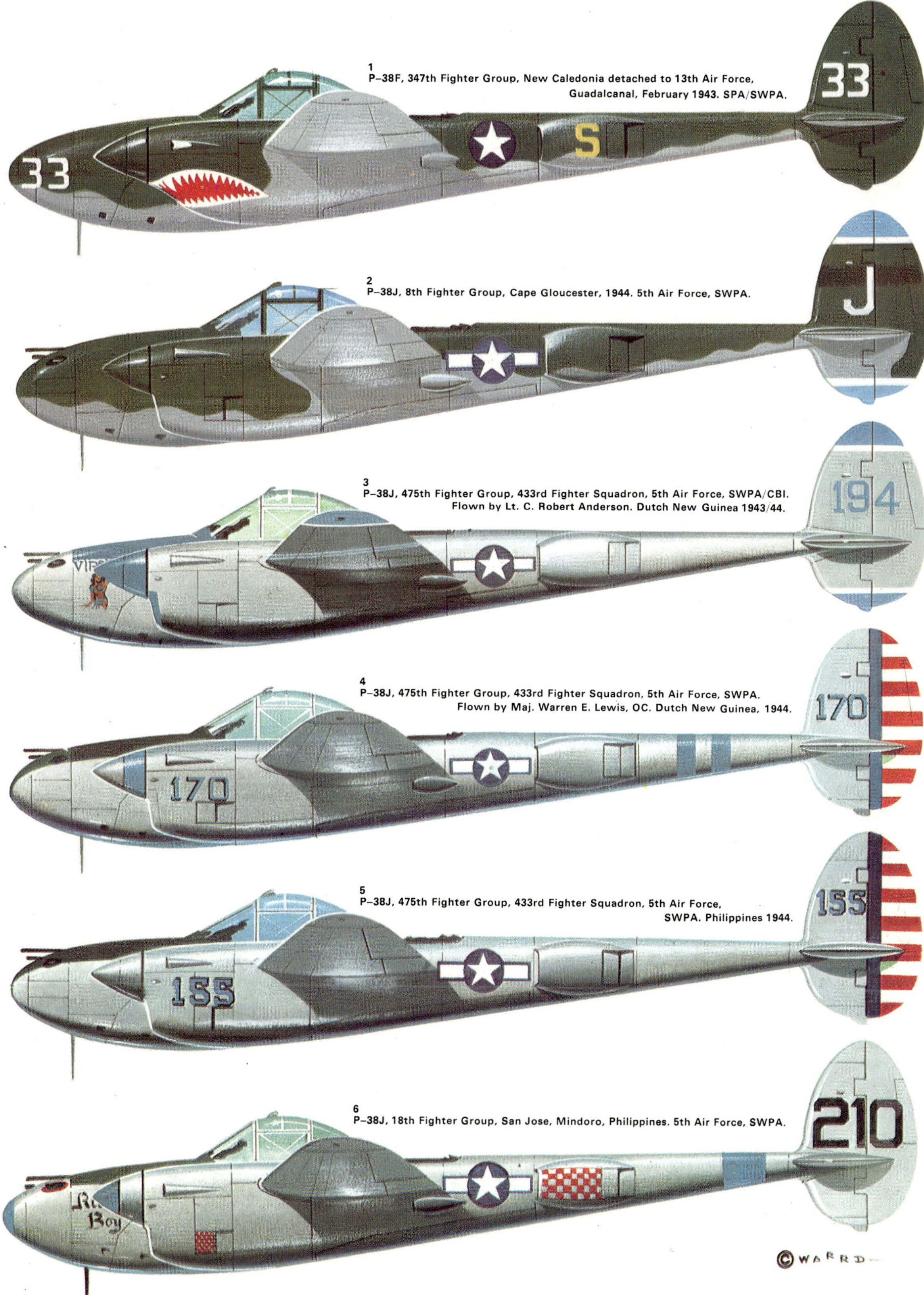

1 P-38F, 347th Fighter Group, New Caledonia detached to 13th Air Force, Guadalcanal, February 1943. SPA/SWPA.

2 P-38J, 8th Fighter Group, Cape Gloucester, 1944. 5th Air Force, SWPA.

3 P-38J, 475th Fighter Group, 433rd Fighter Squadron, 5th Air Force, SWPA/CBI. Flown by Lt. C. Robert Anderson. Dutch New Guinea 1943/44.

4 P-38J, 475th Fighter Group, 433rd Fighter Squadron, 5th Air Force, SWPA. Flown by Maj. Warren E. Lewis, OC. Dutch New Guinea, 1944.

5 P-38J, 475th Fighter Group, 433rd Fighter Squadron, 5th Air Force, SWPA. Philippines 1944.

6 P-38J, 18th Fighter Group, San Jose, Mindoro, Philippines. 5th Air Force, SWPA.

F

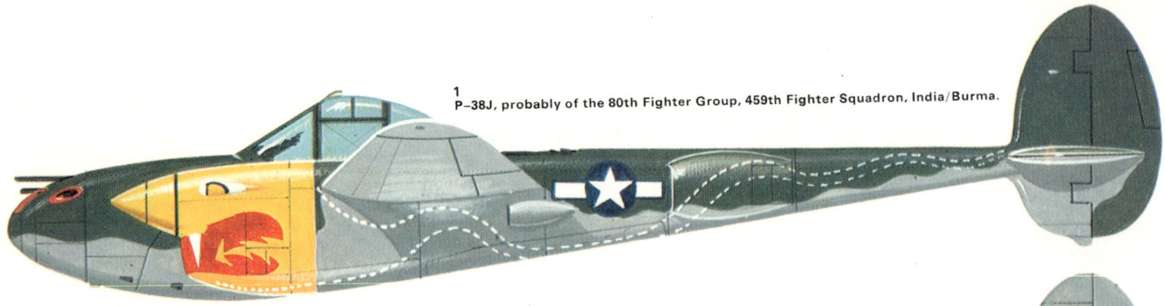

1 P–38J, probably of the 80th Fighter Group, 459th Fighter Squadron, India/Burma.

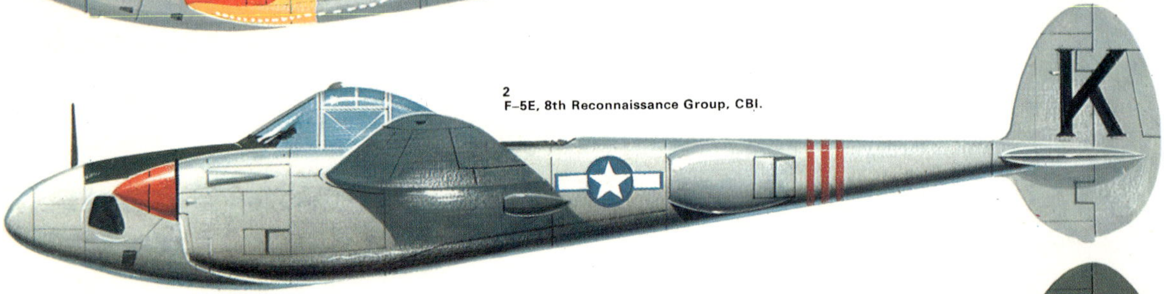

2 F–5E, 8th Reconnaissance Group, CBI.

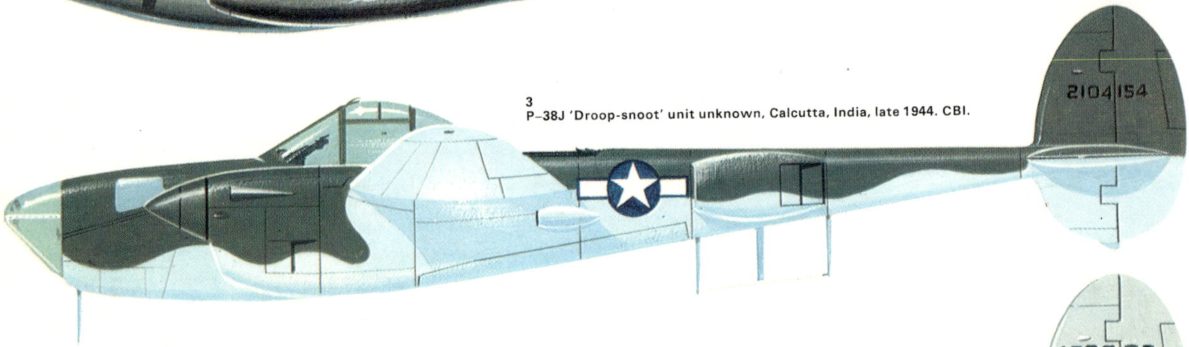

3 P–38J 'Droop-snoot' unit unknown, Calcutta, India, late 1944. CBI.

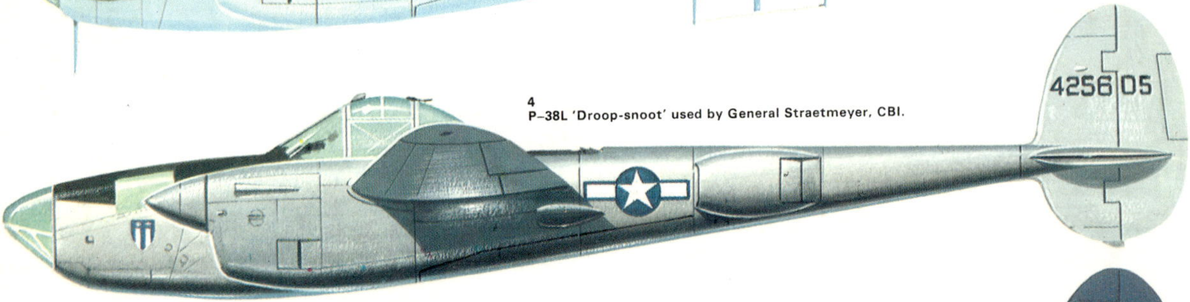

4 P–38L 'Droop-snoot' used by General Straetmeyer, CBI.

5 F–4C, 8th Photographic Reconnaissance Group, India, CBI.

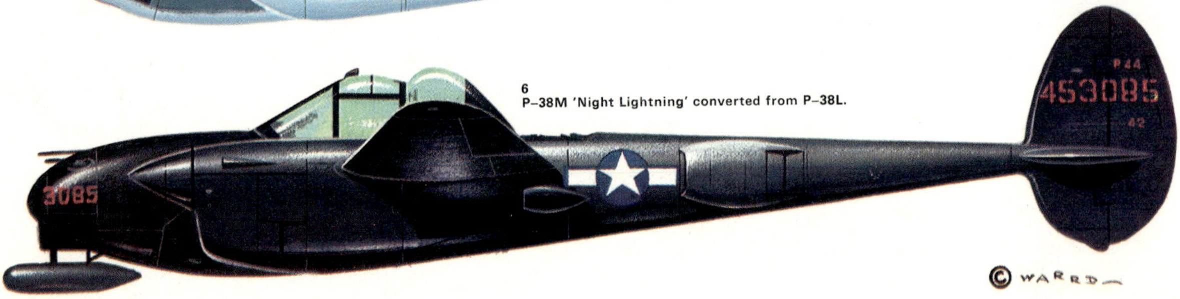

6 P–38M 'Night Lightning' converted from P–38L.

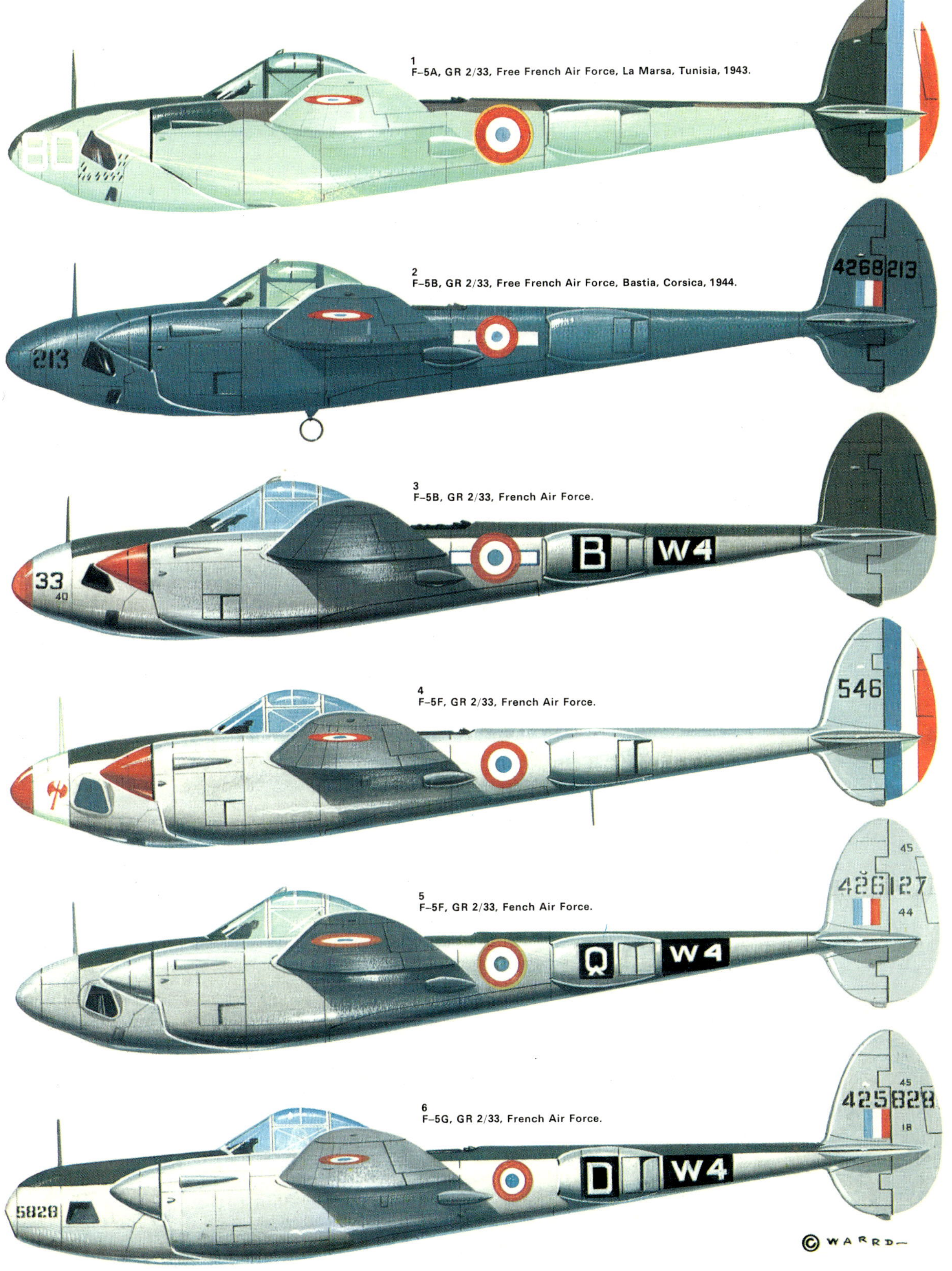

G
1
F—5A, GR 2/33, Free French Air Force, La Marsa, Tunisia, 1943.
2
F—5B, GR 2/33, Free French Air Force, Bastia, Corsica, 1944.
3
F—5B, GR 2/33, French Air Force.
4
F—5F, GR 2/33, French Air Force.
5
F—5F, GR 2/33, Fench Air Force.
6
F—5G, GR 2/33, French Air Force.
WARRD

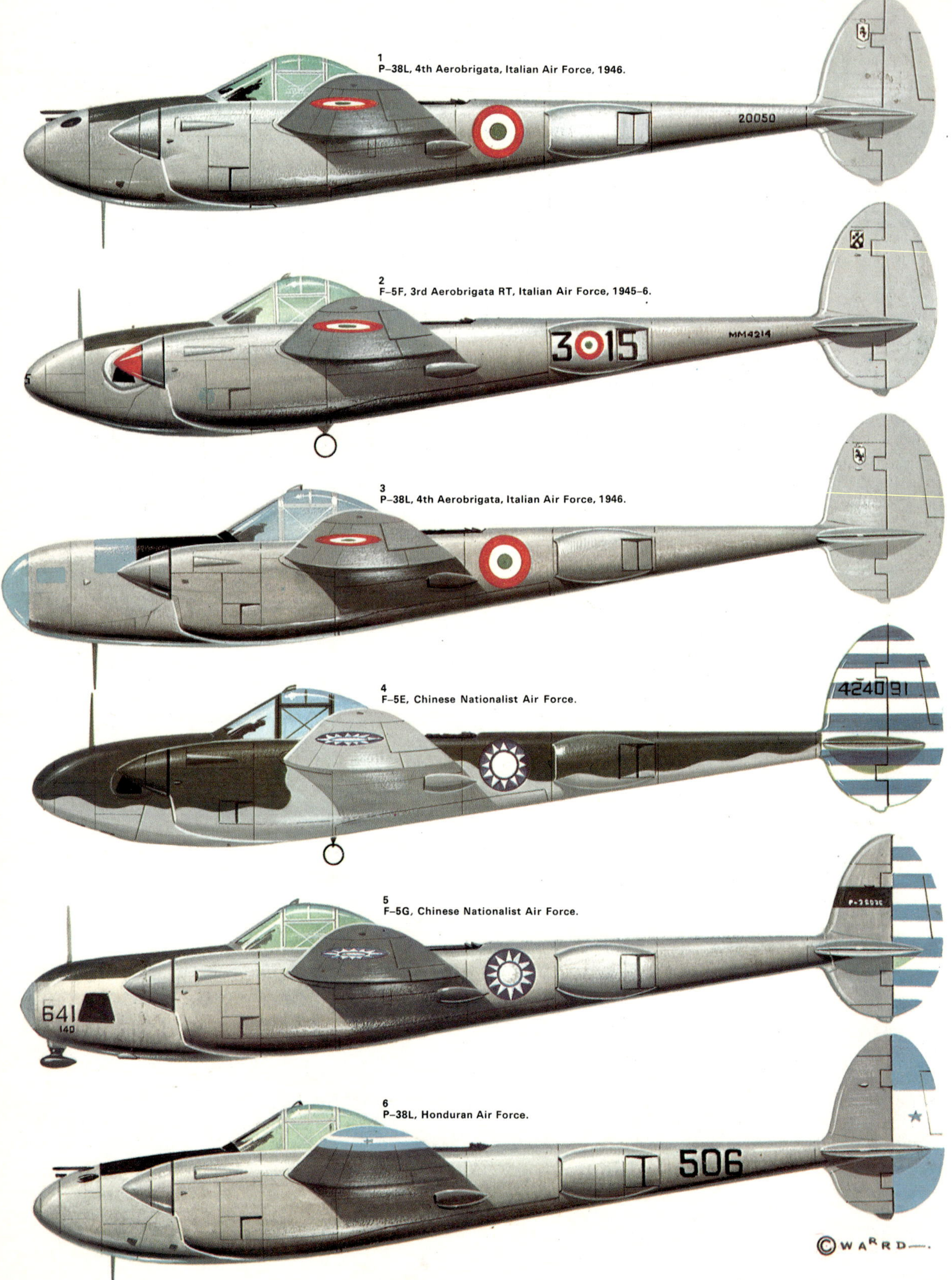

1
P–38L, 4th Aerobrigata, Italian Air Force, 1946.

2
F–5F, 3rd Aerobrigata RT, Italian Air Force, 1945–6.

3
P–38L, 4th Aerobrigata, Italian Air Force, 1946.

4
F–5E, Chinese Nationalist Air Force.

5
F–5G, Chinese Nationalist Air Force.

6
P–38L, Honduran Air Force.

Above: P–38J, 1st Fighter Group, 94th Fighter Squadron, 15th Air Force, Italy, MTO. See colour illustration D5. (USAF)

Left & below: P–38G, 82nd Fighter Group, 97th Fighter Squadron, 15th Air Force, Italy, MTO. (via G. Cattaneo)

Right: P–38G, 82nd FG, 97th FS. The letter C indicated the 97th FS, second letter was the individual aircraft identification letter.
(via G. Cattaneo)

Below: P–38J of an unknown unit nosed over in soft ground at the end of runway on a Yugoslav airfield. (USAF)

Above: P–38J probably of the 80th FG, 459th FS, nicknamed the 'Twin Dragon Squadron'. Note Bazooka tubes, for a change shown on an operational aircraft. CBI.   (USAF)

Below: F–4C, 8th Photographic Reconnaissance Group, at Barrackpur, India, 1944. In background are crated gliders for the 1st Air Commando Group. OD uppers, pale blue unders.   (K. Sumner via J. Sciutti)

Below: F–4C, 8th Photo Recon Group, Pandaveswar, India. PR blue uppers, pale blue unders sprayed into uppers.   (K. Sumney via J. Sciutti)

Below: F–4C, 8th Photo Recon Group, on an Indian airfield, PR blue uppers, pale blue unders, note US ARMY on under surfaces.

(Peter M. Bowers)

Below: F–5A, 8th Photo Recon Group, with an interesting serial, 4–28600, which appears to have belonged to a P–47! Burma, 1944.   (K. Sumner via J. Sciutti)

Below: P–38J 'Droop-snoot' in OD and pale blue camouflage, Calcutta, India, late 1944. Serial No. 2104154.   (Peter M. Bowers)

Above: P–38L 'Droop-snoot' used by General Straetmayer, CBI. (Peter M. Bowers)

Above: P–38L 'Droop-snoot' unit unknown, Calcutta, India, CBI, late 1944. In bare metal finish with white code on black panel and black T on fin and rudder. (Peter M. Bowers)

Right: F–5B, 8th Photo Recon Group, 9th Photo Recon Squadron, India, CBI. February 1945. PR blue overall. (Peter M. Bowers)

Below: F–5B, 8th Photo Recon Group. 9th Photo Recon Squadron, Pandaveswar, India, CBI. Late 1943. PR blue upper surfaces, pale blue under surfaces merging with uppers, note droptanks PR and pale blue. (USAF)

Below: F–5E, 8th PRG, Burma, 1944, Serial 42–67877. (K. Sumney via J. Sciutti)

Above: P–38F, 347th Fighter Group, New Caledonia, detached to 13th Air Force, Guadalcanal, February 1943. See colour illustration.
(Peter M. Bowers)

Above: Line-up of P–38F's of the 347th Fighter Group on Cactus Strip, code word for Henderson Field, Guadalcanal, 1943. First in line 'Little Jo' second 'Fran II'.   (US Marine Corps)
Below: P–38F on dispersal area on a fighter strip near Henderson Field, Guadalcanal. Serial 32239, note RNZAF Kittyhawk in distance. (US Marine Co

Below: A couple of P–38J's taking off from the new airstrip at Cape Gloucester. 8th Fighter Group, 1944, 5th Air Force. SWPA.   (US Marine Corps)

Above & below: Unusual pair of photographs showing a P–38J of the 18th Fighter Group first with starboard then with port engine dead and airscrew feathered, 'Rickie Boy'. (photos Peter M. Bowers)

Left: P–38J of the 475th Fighter Group, 5th Air Force, Philippines. (via E. Munday)

Below: Line-up of Philippine based P–38J's of the 475th Fighter Group. Note OD camouflage has been carried right over the nose. (via E. Vagi)

Interesting shot of a mixed formation of SWPA fighters, P–51D of the 3rd Air Commando Group, P–38J of an unknown unit and the F4U–4 from a squadron of Marine Air Group 31 flying over Honshu, Japan.   (US Marine Corps)

Above: An F–5E of the 28th Photo Recon Squadron, 7th Air Force, dispersed beneath the Palm trees on Ulithi, 24th December 1944. Note 'Avenger' in background.   (US Marine Corps)

Below: Line-up of F–5E's of a 10th Air Force Photo Recon unit on Hangchow field, China, 1945.   (Peter M. Bowers)

Above: A four plane division of USMC Corsairs escort a F–5E swinging in low to photograph a Japanese strong-point in central Okinawa, target was the fortified peak in the middle distance. The Corsairs, plus others out of sight to the left went in with rockets and napalm, the F–5E of the 28th PRS with still and cine cameras. (US Marine Corps)

Left: Same F–5E as above showing the modified long-range tank from which Lt. D. D. Duncan took cine films of Corsair strikes on targets on Okinawa. (US Marine Corps)

Below, two pictures: F–5E of the 28th Photo Recon Squadron, 7th Air Force, coming into land on Yontan airstrip, Okinawa, after recce mission over Kyushu, Japan. (US Marine Corps)

Above: P–38H of the 2nd Service Group, warms up for take-off after a snow storm at Camp Tripoli, Iceland. (USAF)

Above: A pair of P–38F's of the 343rd Fighter Group, 54th Fighter Squadron, 11th Air Force, on a mission out of Longview to Amchitka Aleutians. Note the 54th Squadron insignia on radiator cowls and 'sharkmouth' on 93. (USAF)

Below: P–38G's taxying out for take-off from Unmak airstrip, Aleutians. 343rd Fighter Group, 11th Air Force. (USAF)

Above: P–38H, serial 266923, AAF Tactical Center, Orlando, Florida.   (USAF)

Below: Line-up of Lightnings of a training unit, Santa Maria AFB, California.   (USAF)

Below: Nice flying shot of a P–38L of a training unit.   (USAF)

Detail shots of the P–38M 'Night Lightning'.   (USAF)

Above: F–5A of GR 2/33, French Air Force, La Marsa, Tunisia, late 1943. Green/brown uppers, Sky unders.   (ECA via J. Cuny)

Above & below: F–5B, GR 2/33, French Air Force, in green and brown upper surfaces with sky under surfaces.   (photos ECA via J. Cuny)

Below: F–5F of GR 2/33 on display in Bordeuax.   (J. Cuny)

Above: F—5F of GR 2/33 in bare metal finish but with OD on top of tail booms.   (ECA via J. Cuny)

Above: F—5G of GR 2/33, bare metal with OD tops to booms. (ECA via J. Cuny)

Left: Nose detail of F—5G.   (J. Cuny)

Below: F—5F of GR 2/33 on Dijon airfield.
(S. P. Peltz)

Top: F–5E of the 3rd Aerobrigata, Italian Air Force. Note DF loop under fuselage. (Italian Air Force)

Above: Line-up of P–38J's and F–5E's of the 3rd Aerobrigata, Italian Air Force, 1946. (Italian Air Force)

Right: P–38L, note serial on fuselage, 44–24637 of the 4th Aerobrigata, Italian Air Force. (G. Cattaneo)

Below: P–38L of the 4th Aerobrigata, note 'Cavallino Rampante' insignia on fin. (G. Apostolo)

Above: F–5E, Chinese Nationalist Air Force, Nanking airfield, China, 1946. OD and grey scheme.   (David C. Lucabauch via R. Beuschel)

Above: F–5E, Chinese Nationalist Air Force, Peiping airfield, China, November 1945. Note OD and grey camouflage has been partially removed. Serial 424099, white 03 on nose.   (Peter M. Bowers)

Below: F–5E, serial 424092 on Peiping airfield, China, November 1945.   (D. C. Lucabauch via R. Beuschel)

Below: F–5E's on Kangwan airfield, Shanghai, China, April–Nov. 1946. Chinese serial on OD band on fin P–38033. Note variations in presentation of National insignia and also that it was not the practice to paint the blue and white stripes on the inside of the fin and rudder. (D. C. Lucabauch via R. Beuschel)

Below: F–5G, Kangwan airfield, Shanghai, China, 1946. Chinese serial on OD band on fin P–38036, see colour illustration H6.   (Earl Reinert)

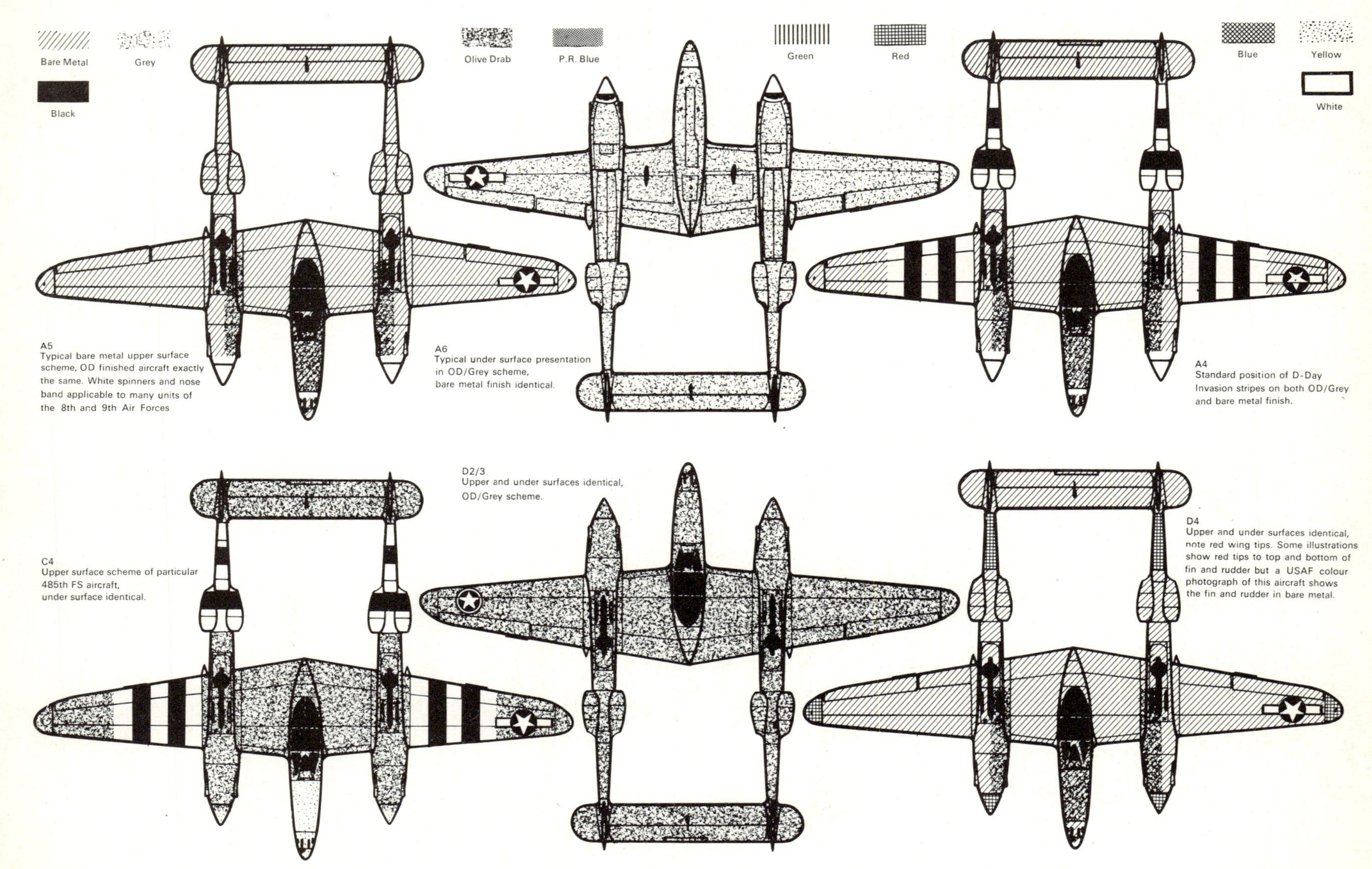

Bare Metal
Grey
Olive Drab
P.R. Blue
Green
Red
Blue
Yellow
Black
White
A5
Typical bare metal upper surface scheme, OD finished aircraft exactly the same. White spinners and nose band applicable to many units of the 8th and 9th Air Forces.
A6
Typical under surface presentation in OD/Grey scheme, bare metal finish identical.
A4
Standard position of D-Day Invasion stripes on both OD/Grey and bare metal finish.
C4
Upper surface scheme of particular 485th FS aircraft, under surface identical.
D2/3
Upper and under surfaces identical, OD/Grey scheme.
D4
Upper and under surfaces identical, note red wing tips. Some illustrations show red tips to top and bottom of fin and rudder but a USAF colour photograph of this aircraft shows the fin and rudder in bare metal.